Unicorn

Penis Envy, and Other Fascinating Sh^t.

Talia V. Scott

Cover Art by Marlon J. Mack
Foreword by Tracy 'Anomaly' Sumpter

Guerilla Spit Literary House

Table of Contents

FOREWORD

When Talia first asked me to write the foreword for *Unicorn Tears, Penis Envy, & Other Fascinating Sh^t*, I wasn't exactly sure where to begin. Having been a friend and fan of her work for over 10 years, I've witnessed what a pen can do in her gifted hands on many occasions. Sometimes it's hard to explain the magic and depth of those closest to you. You're just used to the sparkle and accept it for what it is. But, to quickly understand the writer you're about to journey with, picture the rapper Shyne + writers/poets Edgar Allen Poe, Charles Bukowski, Anais Nin, Alfred Hitchcock and comedian Pee Wee Herman walk into a bar. The bar would probably be that of their favorite mixologist and writer, Talia V. Scott. Why? She can make a drink as you've never had and write the perfect poem to compliment it.

My Drink? "The Unicorn Tear". My Poem? "In the Morning".
A writer's writer, Talia's adeptness for the beautiful struggle of life, has been on display through spoken-word poetry performances across the country for nearly a decade. She cut her teeth on one of South Florida's most well-known stages, The Literary Café, where I served as co-host and workshop co-facilitator. The venue creator, the late Will "Da Real One" Bell, invited her to The Café's Saturday Night Live open mic poetry event + Sunday Stage Therapy writing & performance workshop after seeing her perform at an audition for Malcolm-Jamal Warner in 2008.

At her first workshop, I asked one of my favorite questions of anyone performing at The Café, "Are you a writer, a poet, or a spoken word artist?". I know that she walked in as a writer and blossomed into a spoken word poet.
One of the best the Miracle on 125th Street by way of Baconville(Winston-Salem), N.C. has to offer. It was at the Literary Café that she learned the power of her words. As a "Literary Café Baby" (resident poet) writing with the spirit of "Those Who Labor Here Spit the Truth" and performing to "Be Humble, Yet Explosive."
With this work, her first published book of poetry, *Unicorn Tears, Penis Envy, & Other Fascinating Sh^t,* the timbre and tone of her words will move readers to greater understanding of themselves and the world around them. A Scott poem is a historical, linguistic, and artistic journey. But this is another notch in the belt that is the power of the written word.
Enjoy it, as I did. Share it, as I will.

Tracy "Anomaly" Sumpter
Writer | Event Host | Spoken Word Poet

Unicorn Tears, Penis Envy, & Other Fascinating Sh^t

1
WELCOME TO BACONVILLE

Dirty Mouth

Dirty belly.
A womb disturbed.
Mud-cracked lake and prayer-wall,
Graffitied in the way that stitches scrawled across it
Vast and reticulated
Letters congregate in the cracks
Falling on their knees in an alphabet soup
Confessing & singing about the time this way came a wicked thing.
Call it wounded home to a ghost with little bones whose only haunt
now:
Is memory
Is count,
Hopefully father.
Definitely me.
A disposable bag in a can behind the backdoor of a Parenthood
Unplanned.
Planned.
This was everything but that.
Dirty hands
Forsaken,
Clasped in prayer for forgiveness
And a journey rerouted through a vehicle more fit for it
Attempted replacements
Many moons of sacraments
Alone to atone
For young accidents ending with the infinite consequence of an
inability to forget
Neither of us did.
Dirty mouth.
Rarely speaking of it
Unable to leverage it having happened
Against the reality that none of the things that occurred since would
have without it
I've loaded each of my guns with that dodged bullet
I nail my tongue to the crucifix every time it tenses to speak of it
without regret

Dirty Self.
I testify to churning the mess
With hands fresh, and free, inexperienced & feckless
Desperate.
Bless it.
Belly,
Dust-settled home of tiny ghost
With 'welcome home' sign left written in small print
Hopefully with blessing for the next guest
Dirty feet.
Dragging home to sleep off the events of this reality.

Aries: The Things We Save

Having it all can sometimes be an overrated experience for non-thrill-seekers knowing nothing of what living on the cusp of danger really even smells like...

But,

We are nocturnal,

& this is life.

Fire sign.

We are the chasers of things that may or may not go "bump" in the night.

Take anything that moves:

Disable, conquer, relish, repeat.

We are meat eaters.

& You, elusive

I've often wondered if you're really water,
But still I will chase your tail through the dark

Just to pin it in the morning.

And pin it again in the morning.

Let's just pin it...

That glorious morning.

We are hungry.

Gums quaking from nerves & pang,

Way too old to still be teething but gosh wouldn't it feel great....

For lack of better words....

Strategically wallowing around um..

On some lips??

In a mouth??

Sing this song for me, baby

An ode to the firm nipple of anticipation

Do you know it?

Slow jam with high hat and bass drum?

Sway your hips, please.

Belly,

Museum,

On exhibit, the worlds' oldest most decrepit butterflies on display, fluttering in circles like dummies.

I've got a bug box for you,

But there I cannot watch you fly & my fancy must stay tickled.

Flick your tongue for me,

Aren't we just snakes in the wind?

Smelling it,

Sometimes you just...wanna taste it,

Sometimes you just. want. to taste of it

This,

thing we save.

It's under-fucked & overpaid.

Conversation Before the Mourning

...they say people start to talk in code when death is near...
my granddad asked me to climb into bed with him..
something I hadn't done since I was 6..
and I was tempted...
we played a game of peekaboo,
every time he turned I whimpered
but I'm sure that he knew
every time I dried my eyes & looked over ours met
and although he hasn't left it hurts the fantastic place in my chest
lungs, strong, shuttering to hold back the sobs,
wiping my eyes with the same paper that wiped cheek, chin, & snot
he
cant
see
me. like. this.
he says there's peace for him in the valley
and he
won't let me fix his pillow cuz "only God can fix it" apparently
it's funny...
he randomly tells me to go home & rest
but the only thing I wanna do is hurt beside him in this bed...
the only man who's never cursed me is prepared to leave
and the expectation is for me to be as ready as he,
this is the pretense to the dawn
the conversation before the mourn.
my library is burning &
I can't save the books,
I don't wanna see but I have to look,
all I've ever had is all that it took
this giant has never stumbled,
but now we're at a cliff that overlooks the brook
he says there's peace for him in the valley...
and obviously i can't go.....

he keeps telling me I need rest
.....I wince every time he tells me to go home.
we spoke of Emma & Stella
Puerto Rico & Spain,
someone showing him something
and airplanes...made sure he was comfortable
told him I loved him roughly 6 times...I left...
as he lay.

Ghosted: Day 8

...and then days had passed and she listened to gangster rap & nibbled donuts with her pinky up. Staying classy was the thing...even on the bluest of days when the stars had fallen from the sky and were scraped from beneath the shoes of those watching...

I Don't Belong Here

I find myself treading in the pot I once pissed in
Tossed it onto a shelf to rust while I went on an odyssey saturated with
more funk than laughs without a map
And now that I've found my way I'm
Trying to keep my head up in a solvent made of reality and the dreams
that have seeped from my ear onto my pillow at night that I can now see
without having to be asleep
Sink or swim
They say there's no time like the present
But the fear of drowning is evident
I am liquefied by the sheer fright of peering over this ledge
Yet slowly,
I dribble down the side of my container
Drop by drop
Slowly I overflow
Been thirsting to be thirsted for and sipped
I spill ..
Testing fate as I edge out to the rim
I see a drip pan in the distance
Trying not to waste any of this built up sustenance
Wishing for it to hurry up
Hold onto me tightly this glass I'm in might slip
I sweat at the thought of reaching your lips
Or your chin
Your lap
Sticky on your hands
I'm pouring out on a day soon come overdue
Elusive
Please, God help me with what I shall I do with it
will it hurt when the barrier breaks,
freedom on my face
Freed from the confines of this bottomless fortress
This crate with slick walls

will it ache for but a moment
When I runneth over
Will I be tipped
Long enough for the chapped evidence of this journey to detach
Might it be overwhelming a bit...
To be running when I hit?
The ground, that is
The initial impact of it
The Weight
The gravity
The fear of a splatter regardless of the fact that fail-proof is stamped on
the plans
That my feet have to land
I am filled
And it's requiring all that I have left within me to bridle the advancing tide
behind me
Yet I hunger so greatly
That I'm afraid I'll hurt myself when I'm finally allowed to eat
It'll be a cataclysmic feast of everything
Tsunami
Swallowing beach
No path
Just a systematic monstrosity
And the fact of the matter is that
I am afraid of myself...
And the potential of these thinkable things...
There is no harness for water
The soft
The deep
The waves
The breaks
The rage
This, slow drip,
The heretofore intentions
How have I made it,
While I waded through the catechism and tribulations,
The epochs of waiting and fabricating?
I have conjured an earthquake of such epic proportions
That I've become a mermaid and a contortionist

As this briny deep sea keeps calling me
I bend backward to cast back the damp clique of undercurrents with one
hand
And with the other I paddle
There are ripples surrounding me in this water
And fear isn't great enough to stop it
Clash of the Titans
Something wicked this way comes
And it's a flash flood of all my sweat, guts, and blood
Yes I asked for this
Yet the closer that it gets
I grow suspicious
Staring at my reflection in the mirror asking it questions to make sure she
is not a con-artist or pretender
The password is: commitment
God give me wisdom and remembrance
Savoir faire and turbulence
Allow me to keep my lawlessness
When the falls comes crashing down on my back and my feet come to
rest...
On the bottom

Rise

It's 4am and I realized for the umpteenth time that I've fallen down again,
Again and again and again
I,
Realized that that ol quote about having been buried but they didn't know
I was a seed
Has a few more requirements to meet,
See,
My dirt ain't wet.
I need the sun to shine a lil piece of lil ray on me
Can I get some pollen and a lil bumble from a bee on me
It ainteem been spring lately...
But certainty has guaranteed me that if I slip 9 times and I decide to get up
10
There will come a mighty wind and a storm and a shift and a shake and
little, heavy metal and gospel, and jazz, and a symphony of cryin
Besides the ground ain't nothin but a big ol desk for writing what I'm
gonna do and planning how I'll bloom
Jotting down details about my petals and their shade of blue
I'll write a haiku about how no one will pluck me because they love me
and the best way to show is to let grow
I'll weather storms and stay firmly rooted ain't no place for me in the most
elegant of vases
So I'll keep two thorns just in case
They're gonna need a band for me when I stand
Please, just leave me laying here dirty and unkempt
Denied and deprived
So I can rise.

It's 4am and I realized for the umpteenth time
that the best to ever say it was Anäis Nin who wrote,

"I'm restless. Things are calling me away. My hair is being pulled by the
stars again."

And everybody won't believe

Some of these people mighteem leave
I could be behind or ahead
I could be late and early
I could be the tortoise and the hare
The race is between my mind and my feet
The plot could thicken or totally dissipate
And while the resources might evade me as long as I'm on the ground I
retain the propensity to get up
As surely as the sun rises there will also be a lil dusk
Maybe I'll write a lil song inspired by lightening bugs, and shootin stars,
and night lights, and taking chances, and seeing things through, and
maybe I'll write about the importance of the dark
And everybody won't believe
Some of these people mighteem leave
If you knew the pillowtalk someone lying low was capable of you too may
never sleep again
And you too might lie awake at night dreaming and writing your things
Stacking them high,
High,
High,
20 ft taller at the end of this
Stack your things high,
So we can rise.

Places

But in here I'm just a nigga
Just the girl with nappy hair
Just the brown one
Just the loud one
Just the one who thinks she's invincible cuz if I don't who will?

The Quarantine File #1

On, or about, the 8th day
Some of the Christians and Jews
Buddhists, Muslims, Hindus
And even a few of the spiritually unenthused started preparing rituals &
gathering their tools.
By way of the chant,
The prayer,
An offering of incense and/or fruit
To bless their doors & daughters
With smudges from thumbings of oil that they'd blessed themselves
Because preachers weren't going door to door.
It was the strangest thing for those who stopped to think
That the multitudes had been brought to their knees
When that little ol contagion was crowned King.
But the people,
The people continued to smudge with their thumbs the blood of lamb that
they'd also chop on wooden blocks or sauté on stove tops If they're fancy,
Or privileged,
Or simply chasing normalcy when the only destination left without a ban
on travel is in the cuisine
Because we can get lost there.
Even when some of us still can't eat.
We can spend the day defiling the wall that was built to bring difficulty to
duality
And if you ask me,
Only if you ask
I'd say it seemed like a lil taste of synthesis
The others did the work of rejoicing in the midst of the circumstance
Have you ever heard of Exodus?
Late into the night the music men gave us rhythms and reasons to hooray
and dance
It was the clang of deserted streets and seats emptied of asses with
nowhere to go but home
Had us in there before the streetlights came on
It sat down and found somewhere to be still
In the sound of silence
Put out the fiercest of fires

Keep a shallow rooted tree upright while the rest of the forest falls
It can make a cloud talk
In the wake of drum beat in sync with the strike of Apache feet
There were some who took to their balconies,
And the streets,
The cul de sacs,
And porches with their horns
And voices,
Because slowly an eclipsing epiphany covered occurred to those that were listening that this might be a cleansing
Well overdue
So they gathered their things
Fumbling through the pantries
And running back to the place that they keep the groceries to see if everyone had overlooked the ritualistic herbs, oils, and meats
Repeat,
After about a week into the unforeseen I saw some the Christians and some of the Jews
Had brought back that old thing...
They'll smudge their doors to protect their sons and daughters
As the new Crowned King of the month came near
So that ol' plague would reconsider entering here
Call it what you wanna
But we've been here before
Call it legend, tradition, lies and lore
It'd started looking more and more like something or somebody had come to settle score
And maybe it was Motha Fuckin Nature seeking some restoration and sending everyone to their rooms without their dinner...

Scream:
Ode to Allen Ginsberg: *Howl*

I've seen insecurity deem fearlessness as being crazy.
There's construction underneath the roof tops
Being conceived from the ground up,
And every time a giant stumbles
I recall that I, too, have dropped.
So prepare for the ram beneath a full moon in the back drop.
WIth authenticity in the recipe,
Being engineered from scratch,
Ramming trees & skinning skin from the bark for building the building and the fucking parking lot.
For every two people who think insanity is what lies beneath what I don't even deem to be creative things,
Just shadow puppets and verbalizations of the thing in which I believe,
There are four who think I'm a fucking goddess.
Regardless,
I have watched friends who hate themselves enough for loving cock to camouflage the cum spots with fraternal bands of love for non-blood related brethren with cocks.
Whoa to the mysterious ways of God.
Call the kettle black and it's still a pot.
I have watched the unraveling of strange-fruit in the bedroom of apartment 202.
A beautiful creature filled with self hate, asphyxiated, hanging, from the canopy of his bed,
Avoid the smell of flesh.
Agony of defeat.
He had the compassion to turn down the A/C in hopes to curb the horror of the others who would discover him, after several days, in the midst of the summer haze.
Though maybe,
A last minute perversion could've been the case
As he was ticketed for the plane and by his door sat his suitcase.
Ode to the dread of being in the presence of those whose lips mime thoughts that many men wish upon a star to even dream of
Proudly wreaking of what you think stinks because of the inability to own the stench of being real.

Hurt feelings were made from seeking attention, like heat-seeking missiles, real broken heart commit suicide, rise, and travel the dimensions for recognizance.

The fuck your feelings Phoenix.

They are ferry boat captains for the river Styx.

For dream killers & dicks.

For assholes & dicks.

I've seen tricks with high hopes in search of a golden road delving into the unknown abyss.

I've seen in Dorothy in an alley stained yellow with pestilence & piss

Allowing men with chains & whips to douse her Toto in Aristocrat, Ciroc, or Crys.

I've seen losers who succeed.

Christians who rarely drop to their knees.

Writers unable to read or speak,

All lost in the circumstance of being caught up:

in being a bystander

in being a bitch who's only skill is being fertile

in being accused of being deep because others simply can't swim

in being a high functioning mute.

I've seen men who put their cocks on the tongues of the wicked.

This is an Ode to the dread of when their balls start itching.

I neglected to mention that this is why men think that they're gods;

Baring more women from the tips of their heads than Zeus ever could giving birth to Athena.

I have watched beautiful disasters like ugly babies filled with laughter

And arrogant bastards

Like you.

2
RAINY DAY GIRL

Isadora

"I will always be the virgin-prostitute, the perverse angel, the two-faced
sinister and saintly woman."
-Anais Nin

I fell knowing fully well you'd turn your back at the crash
Hid your hands
And I've now got cracks
I thought for certain that I was in ruins
Until on my journey I stumbled upon an old witch's mountain with a view
An old witch with a brew for a bitch that would last for Miles
I'll never forget the day this,
Old woman the, last Doyen of Kintsugi
Sold me the last of the gold meant for minding broken bowls
Said it bound back together broken souls
She said...
I'm worth more distorted from the circumstance
Of thinking I might go to sleep in the box you built for me.
It's taking longer for my fingernails to regenerate lately.
Left,
Generations of fingertips in slick surfaces from trying to escape
They break,
Popping loudly in the key of beloved
Loud like a snap in the Church house

The blow that I was dealt had the audacity to sit there,
Indian-style
Like child,
Arms folded,
Temper tantrumesque,
Deeply embedded in my chest.
What a mess.
Pocketed and deep
Stress fractured,
I've seen prettier potholes etched into the streets
I've seen canyons,
Filled with water deep,

With ledges still fertile enough to bare trees
I've dipped down to my knuckles in that metallic slurry
Legend says the touch of old King Midas has been reignited in me

I am the last last Doyen of Kintsugi
They call me....Isadora

Am I Not a Princess?

Am I Not a Princess?
You've never seen sweetness because the glasses you wear for me are
salt-rimmed,
decorated with barbed wire & burning sage,
All favors for a party I never knew was mine

You taste-test me with a condom on your tongue for desensitization
purposes,
Afraid of the raw, the dirty, the crave, the tang, the smack, the burst,
the penchant
and wonder why your perception is askew

Am I not a princess?

Miniskirts & the evidence of curves are reserved for days that 'frisky' is
more than a brand of cat food,
& eagerness awakens for the moment your face tells tale that you'd
forgotten I could look like that

Am I not icing?

Am I not a princess because my distress is never advertised & any
requests for a savior pass over the pile on your desk,
This... is what my father is for

On the innermost side of delicate lips is a mouth riddled happily with
profanity,
Flowered about like a garden of shell-casings
They say this means I'm honest...
You once loved the smell of gun powder.

Fact: certainty is femininity's ugly cousin.
Fact: decision-making is a masculine trait.
Fact: these facts in fact have no factual basis.

Am I not dark berry?

Am I not juice?
Am I not shortcake?

You have felt my confection more times than it has dusted over the
center of your crosshairs,
& sprinkled across your ears,
The sorbet of it all lives in what I do, not in what I say

The jaggery exists for authenticity, behind cupboard doors,
Easily accessible to those who seek it just beware,
The kitchen is often hot.
The kitchen is often hot.
The kitchen,
Is often,
hot.

Feather

Forget that I ever existed
I left a 1st floor window open for you but the only thing that ever came in
was the breeze and whatever it happened to carry in with it
Most days it would only be a piece of the curtain riding in
Maybe the repetitive hum of a bug's wings
The tap of their feet
A dryer sheet,
My neighbors tend to do laundry on Saturday mornings
Other days it was a used band aid come to cover your wound
Shape-shifted into beard-gang and loc
Needing me
I crafting "we"
Taking me gifts of nothing but advantage and cock
Yes, breezes and cock they
Come and they go
Out like the trash
Traffic
Dirtying up my curtain
While I waited for you
The one who was never coming
Always there yet never walking
Grasping my hand but only holding
Left my window open for you
At night in the dark
During the day when I was away
I wrote a letter to the wind
Sent singing telegrams to falling stars
I sang lullabies to airplane exhaust trails
Thinking one of them would set adrift my memory
I threw line & reel hoping to catch your brown eyes in the spring drizzle
But the unremitting rain ruined my carpet
I'm sure I'll lose my deposit
I'm sure I have lost my deposits
You are too heavy now
With your cement feet
And long face

I cannot carry a chisel & hammer to pry a feather from a block
When I've seen you perch and prance with your flock
I've seen you atop quill pens
And fill pillows
You've tickled noses
And traced the skin of crocodiles with big tears like it was porcelain, like it was nothing
I left my window open for you
So wide that anyone and everyone has drifted in
And I grinned
Welcoming the particles of dust and debris
Happily behind them I would clean
One day, I knew, you, it would be
Yet this dawn I've realized that I'm gone
And the only flowers you ever gave me are these poems & songs
Did you know
I've got a moat around my window...
A deep trench of filth and moisture
And bags, I refuse to carry
And sad, I refuse to marry
And mad, I cannot ferry any further in a storm named for you
I've got rotted wood
And poisonous snakes that want to slither in
But the clouds tell me you're fine
A little dark over yonder from time to time
Yet otherwise fine
No signs of you looking for me
Don't want no
Comfort & understanding
Don't want no
Loving
Forget I ever existed
Don't wish upon stars for me
Don't ask for peace during your prayers between the ground and your knees
Cuz I've asked God plenty
And he told me to set adrift upon a memory
Where did you go, tempest?
Where did you go, gale?

Where did you go, little gust?
Baby, I've got to close it
And once I'm gone I won't know your name
Oh baby, I've got to close it
And once it's done it won't be the same
Won't you just,
Slip through while time still remains
Won't you just,
Slip through and help me clean up the stains

Sun in Aries/Moon in Scorpio

I

I shouldn't have suffocated my love...
Let off the gas long ago and stowed it away in an unsafe container
Waiting for a storm of haling alarm clocks & rain
Should've known it would blow someday...
It's to be expected that with the confetti of chaos embedded in your face
I would be the prime suspect for feloniously packing these gallons too tightly anyway
I've got a habit of dropping lit matches...
In the middle of spills...
I fancy the perfume of flammable liquid...
...watching to see how long the pyre can breathe
I've been covered in soot plenty.
But I've been working on my respirations though as not to get my lungs involved in the debauchery of my fire-starting activities
They call me "Aries"....
The incubator of gross completion or nothing
...they say I've got a tendency to live my life in extremes.

II

I've always loved to play with water...
So calm and serene...
But beneath the surface I know your eddy is chafed and seething
And I'd...
Simply like you to come out and play with me
But seemingly you have no interest with your labored patience of a monk
So for refusing me I'll simply stand on your shore...daringly...
Provoking your stream
Skipping rocks off your head,
Trying to chip your teeth
Get real big,
Get real big and quicken into a torrent for me...
Just this once, please ...
Wanna see how bad it bothers you
...This bullshit tranquility cannot distract nor puzzle me

Together since we were mere flicker and puddle
I'm your favorite beast,
Now feed me...
But this is the point...
Refrain from giving me my sustenance and meat
Hold hostage the tub from which I receive my Adam's ale steep
You know...
What you're doing
Punish me...
Frigid waters percuss with the same precision as a scorpion's sting
I see...
I waded on your bank last night under the cobalt gloss of moon & in a
school of fish I caught that epiphany,
Did you see me when I did it?
You reflect light so beautifully, my sweet
Take that mask off though, baby
You know I fucks with you ugly
Let me see that murk
...wipe you clean

Missing You

They say that joy comes in the morning,

And the plague is all in your head,

They never bother to tell you the nights' mighty long when the one you're mourning ain't even dead...

There's a reaper that brings the river Styx to wherever I be,

Here you come during my thrills, my sleep, and even my eat

He delivers you on his dinghy.

Crashing against the waves,

There's creepy asylum in knowing that there's no safe passage through any of my days.

Incapable of savoring something as simple as a taco without contemplating your face.

A motherfucking taco!

I take sips of cocktails with a nod to the debauches gone by.

I find difficulty recalling many a happy time without falling into the abyss and splashing around in your dreamy eyes.

I tend to wonder if it's bothersome;

That your spirit wanders to me without your permission often.

I tend to tell him my desires,

That I want my things back

Your heart, your ease, the savage, and the fire.

<u>This Old House, These Old Bones</u>

No longer exposing necks & bellies in submission, the paint is cracked, chipping
& I want you, on me, adorning thee like poppy flowers on collars, over yonder, across the water, on Remembrance Day
I beg of you, to recollect the good things, & the ways, we once placated each other's faces with delicate gestures of the hand
and now those have all but been banned, since you, decided that its best if you refrain from resting your head upon my breast because matters of the heart are best left on the chest
& you'd rather not die there. You'd rather not die there leaving a chalk outline of your ear, jaw line, and hair
near my nipple, heart, or lung,
denying the fact that suckling at my teat while syncopating your breaths with my heart beat leaves you satiated & young
ode to the offerings of your lips & tongue once left at the altar to which you clung
move, watch, rest, breath
deflect, the bullshit on me because you don't trust the process of allowing us to coalesce,
more or less,
you've self prescribed indoctrinated medications that have yet to ease the pain of the past, this won't last if you ask
I've got, two legs instead of four which why there's piss poor performance with this sport, of feline & rodent games
it's a shame,
at times I wonder if you even recall my name
everything I'm not saying is scribbled across my face and contained within long gazes.
to anybody who ever wondered, to anybody who ever cared, for anybody who ever walked down corridors of stone & mortar shielded from elements & harsh winter air
have we ever paid homage to the palisade? The brick mason or the layer?
the precipice of the walls are falling, wishing for a fresh coat over chipped, flaking skin every time the light flicks and your beautiful soul walks in
they scream for you, through dust & remnants of sticky finger prints from

careless hands gripping them, tickling them for their own feckless sensory fulfillment

sand it down and refurbish this shit, but you off & go

finding more beauty in picket fences, with them being nothing more than decorative yard bitches

yet where is the protection?

the neglect to mention that I, shield you from the rain

contain your cries of fury, delicacy, & pain

but who weeps for me?

no sympathy when winter creeps and ice water seeps through the rooftop

& the cleaves, you leave, and stick a fucking pot underneath to catch the leaks

occasionally I moan & creek while you sleep but of course you think that I'm just contracting & settling in the summer night's heat

but it's me, crying out for you

aching to be coated in a substratum of chocolatey almond milk goodness akin to

Macchiato crushed cocoa honey & Kona coffee in a cacophony of cooked bronze-before-dawn stew, soup, syrup

I'd even bask in a barren batter of your bitter thinner

submission, our necks & bellies no longer uncovered for one another to marvel at, over, nor under

dimming this light does not put asunder the chemical reaction that happens when you, put yourself, on. me.

Single

a cup of unrequited love runneth over...

it's a slow death &

there have been many coffins prepared for me...

diggin to the depths,

feverishly writing notes to self

"where's my epic lover" or "where's the help?"

it's strictly bullshit directly from beneath the tail...

it smells..

i stopped flicking coins into wishing wells

shitting in one hand tends to fill quicker and

it paints a picture...

that my wants have been reduced to faith in nickel or copper,

flipped by the tip of a forefinger hoping a high power grants it

before impact cracks and it oxidizes in the water

no,

my penny won't be sent to the slaughter,

won't,

be a martyr, oh

i'd rather be an escape artist.

fantasy houdini in my dreams,

protect my fantasy & feeling

suspend me from the ceiling,

give me pen, parchment, and 10 minutes to rewrite this scene

and escape the memory

....of being chronically single.

Church

You'll never be able to sit in the back of that Church

Watching him bide his time at the end of an aisle traveled by merely a body cloaked in a dress, white,-washed

Tick tock

There are times when you tell your best friend that the only way you'll be in attendance at his wedding is if he's meeting you at the altar

That night, in the dark

Cast your egos to the sidewalk

These, these are conversations had at 3am in the front seats of cars

Splendid, underneath the watchful eye of the stars

A Denzel Washington - Glory type of tear in a low-crawl sneaking down your cheek

Barely drunk

Far from sober

Cigarette smoke

A concoction of emotions

He'll tell you things that you'll keep secret

He'll tell you things you already knew

Selective about the bits of history that are still relevant

And committed to what makes the cut

Crossroads

No signals

No road signs

No wind bringing the scent of anything familiar

There are times when you wanna bury your head in his chest

These are the things you realize when you're not so certain that time has been on your side

But you know letting your truth go at the sound of the gun is

And you'll run fast but steady

There are times when you realize a boy has become a man

And now his hands can swallow yours

And now he tells you you hurt him

And now you realize that he's still fine with no signs of turning back

There are times when you tell your best friend you've been lying to him

For years...

And that doubt no longer reaps the benefit in here

It's time, you tell him

To make hard decisions that he'll either love you or hate you for

And you're prepared for either one because your heart literally can't breathe with this noose around its necks

You'll tell him you're stepping off the stool

You'll tell him, you have 1/2 hung happily there

For too long

And the pump has become a flutter

You'll tell him you're foot is slipping and oh what a gift it'll be to cut the rope

Tell him he can catch you if he so wishes

You'll tell him, you've watched way too many movies about this and refuse to make the same mistakes that those bitches did

You'll tell him

Everything

Shit he shouldn't know

Shit you didn't know you'd say

You'll forgive him before he even says he's sorry because you know that he is

And you'll tell him that this line he's drawn in the sand has got to go

You'll tell him you're a rip tide

You'll tell him you're the high tide

You'll tell him you're the one

You'll tell him you're the pull of the moon

And God keeps saving him for you

You'll ask him to see, and see, and see

Things he should've seen

Then see

But you won't plead...

You'll only say these things once...

You'll ask him to think...

You'll tell him how long you've been trying to make wrong shit right

You'll tell him you're feeling wildly fucking dangerous even showing up here tonight

You'll look at him like he's a night-blooming flower and the way the night sky is hitting his skin is simply toxic

He will open

But you will not pick him because to love is to let grow

You'll tell him that he's been cut enough though...

And the redolence of his sorrow mixed with these leather seats and Courvoisier stained tongues is turning you on

You'll tell him that he'll live forever regardless because you can't stop writing poems...

Like this.

<u>Open Mic</u>

I'm leaving the mic on for you,

Center stages

On pages

I've left my last word

Left my last hurt

Got pressure belly-up in my chest from this next verse

Wouldn't wish it on my nemesis,

Nothing worse

This,

Slow convulse of predilection

Can't let go,

You went away

Yet somehow we both stay

In this place

With moving walkways

Sometimes the direction... is the same

Sometimes we bypass one another for what seems like eternal moonlight nailing glances into each other's face

We keep bypassing gates with open seats

On planes

Wanna just fly away

With you

With you

Fly away

Here we can't stay

Look what remains

Deep cuts full of ashes from the flames

We flick lit matches at each other's feet

Pouring gas in the wound to make us dance

But really, you just needed me to take 10 steps back

My god renders you powerless and distracted

We stand in this air rampant with soot,

dying black

Set my lungs ablaze just to avoid inhaling your handsome perfume,

Nose exploding with the plume of exhausted passion

Inaction

Wanna ravage your body under the watchful eye of daylight

Make the moon cry

Love so merciless one thrust of your back,

One crash of your hand will crack open the sky

Like a unripened peach busted open by your thumb's grasp

Cause the stars to let go an envious sob

We so high

I,

Still so low

I'm leaving the mic on for you

Gotta go all the way,

Walk off into the audience to tell you

Gotta make sure you know none of this is for the play

It ain't entertainment purposes nor noise-cancelling lifejacket for airwaves

This is medicinals entrapped in motion light on stage

My muse

My chaos

My confetti and my news

Not sure what to do

I'm tired I'm exhausted

It's debilitating loving little me some all of you

Without boundary

Without noose

Unconditionally

Don't care 'bout your hidden colors and moods

I been blue

Enough for me and for you

Been black

And I've been bruised

I'm leaving the mic on for you

Want you up out of that seat

Want you to speak

Don't want you to leave the expo satisfied

Don't want the passenger seat in the charcoal chariot tonight

Want you backstage

Want you after the show

After the pictures are taken and numbers exchanged

Want a private show from the one who lives infinitely in the front row

My dream

My beam

My grievance my gloom

Nobody here but me and you

Never been anybody here except little me and big ol you

I'm leaving the mic on for you

I gotta disappear from your view if this is the night you've decided to be mute

I can see it clearly but, heavenly, I've got to hear you

Need you to gasp for me from the mouth that isn't there

Need to know if you're drowning with me before I take my mask off and catch a breath of this foreign air....

He Prayed

He prayed for the rain...
So I tucked the storm neatly in my cheeks before I came
Opened my mouth for him most fiercely on cloudy days
But he didn't know what to do with all the water.
I offered an umbrella but that only made it harder...
Could've sworn in his sleep he'd called upon the floods,
I presumed him too free to mind wet feet...
So I,
Inundated the ground with beads of me to provoke his roots,
I'll be damned, gather roun', y'all, told me I'd forgotten to bring his boots
Gather roun', y'all, told me I'd asphyxiated his roots
He invoked the acrimony of spring...
& had the audacity to deny the bud & the bee,
I asked him,
"What you call me for, lover?"
"What you call me for, dear man?"
"Thought you'd called on me to bring the heat,
I arrived with the nitro & the breeze,
I got up and put clothes on to come & fertilize yo' seeds
Stuck Kentucky Blue in my teeth & St. Augustine 'tween my knees,
And I'll be a slug on a sidewalk salty that
Unbeknownst to me,
You summoned the monsoon to come and keep the unattended scorch
company.
I could've sworn, delight...
I could've sworn when I took gang gang bike rides with the wind...
I know for a fact, puzzling beast,
that when I spent nights afoot journeying with bare feet in the barbed
halls of your ill-constructed mind,
Gashing my fingers on the Braille you left made of shiv & thorn & other
sharp shit that lined your lines,
You conjured the storm,
A fruited baptism for the juiceless,
With musical arrangements composed by Chiquita-fucking-banana & 'nem

Just to repudiate the aches of your pains,
the needs of your seeds,
Y'all, he rose from his knees...
Walked his pasture floor with me just to cover it with smokescreen &
drain,
He prayed for the rain...
Just to layer the land with water-resistant shield & pottery,
T'was trickery,
Trailed off to a whisper in his chant,
Promise I never heard him sing,
'Just come take a walk with me,
Hold hands with thee,
Might get thirsty on my journey,
Dehydrated,
Don't know how to drink,
Might be lonely & starve a little,
Need a nourishing.
I've got feathers,
All-weather,
Bind up your solvent,
Then cast it off of me,
I've got an allergy to your nature
Can't digest your tea,
Storm,
Come come
Just keep me company..."
He prayed for the rain...

3
TO MURDER A MUSE

Muse Murder Music

The crowd...
They will rest easy in their seats.
They will not wince.
Instead they will look on in approving delight,
Instead they will cheer,
They will sneer
The angry mob is deep,
At the colosseum in the nosebleeds
Ringside with Iron Mike
In the jungle
Wait, for the rumble
Corner seat at the octagon,
Rise to your feet when the crowned king takes the lick that makes him
shit his teeth
Under the big top when the lions go rogue,
Trampled when the crowd goes home
This is deeper than death-match
That's good.
Stay there.
The score for this saga,
a soured reminisce of 80's soft rock and the repetitive quake of Angela
Bassett's feet walking against a cigarette-flick
With particular attention paid to the way the pebbles jump around her
feet as she leaves.
And you are the gladiator that failed them.
Their sweetheart,
The disappointment.
And I with this pen am patiently waiting for their thumbs to turn,
This is the scene they call "suspense",
Because I'm going to make you watch their decision from the reflection
in my eyes,
Welled with tears because I've got to murder you to save myself,
My,
Love

My,
Poison
I look to them,
Give me a signal
To end this motherfucker right now
Not soap opera + action movie style,
With a smile and finesse
It never occurred to me that me and my pen are the only reason you've
been allowed to live
I forgot that when a writer loves you, you can live forever
It never occurred to me until this early morn that I'm one gripping the
ink-dipped dagger
Pick your poison, baby

Becoming One

I've been a forfeiture of my voice when it comes to singing these songs about how I long

Long for love like I've been looking for it in all the wrong places

Like I forgot my hiding places

While I was seeking to find faces to replace the one like yours and yours

That I'd lost or mishandled or misplaced

And lately I've started to dissociate.

Disconnecting from the frivolous bindings of our energies that collapsed every time I tried to tap a cap for good luck before we drank

My mistakes,

See none of them were ever mine so they couldn't have been taken

In exchange for my grace I was given a clean slate by which to exchange glances with a new man without the horror of having to hesitate and pray

In exchange for my grace the price I've had to pay though

Has been becoming fuck boy enemy #1 of the state

I've studied the tricks of every play and every day

I reflect on the failed expectations of trying to love deeply in the shallow depths I keep

Keeping mementos of the substitutions of intimacy in my phone

In my bones

Meaningless exchanges and embraces disgraced from the beginning

I keep

Keeping mementos of the intricacies if intimacy

I keep

I keep keeping on

Writing ballads for someone else to croon about my adventures in going unpicked by the lowest hanging fruit

What's the use when everybody I keep picking is a reflection of you?

What lies beneath

Let's get to the root;

It was always midnight in my garden of begging your pardon

In every space I leave packed bags by the door

I gotta gon and head back to the house after I leave the bedside of my newest muse

And await the moment he, too, makes me bleed

Untitled

...I've been mourning you.

And grieving someone who's still alive comes with the company of an unnatural genre of ghost...

A constant haunt.

And I'm having a ton of trouble trying to pray this thing off

The be-ever-presence of your heartbeat won't depart from me upon request the same way in Jesus' name as the energy of the deceased do

They, just come to visit

Yet you, on the other hand have the energy of something that's highly pissed

Something unfinished

Preferring to put mask and love-me-not to it

Don't wanna deal with it

But regardless of the fright you inflict

In my sleep I've perfected a way to remain perfectly still as not to wake because the truth of these matters is that this is the only avenue to meet something missed

Lately I've often worn black..

I've been asking the universe to hire an assassin..

But apparently there's no bold face with sharp enough teeth to take a snag at it

I keep trying figuratively to drop a duo of roses on your casket

But there's a 3inch thick sheet of plexiglass blocking my attempts at it.

I've even tried stitching explosives to their petals

Yet it blows back nothing but my breath and my hair

Sets me back 4 steps

Sets me back 4 steps

Knocks rock & chalk from my grip

I play hop-scotch just to measure how far I've gotten

Inconsolably restless

While you've selected to dead it

Buried yourself in a box without doors that I can't seem to ingress

This,

Has everything it requires for the premise of something going awry

To the same rhythm as something going "thump" in the night

How long will I stand here knocking?

Concocting doorbells out of dynamite in a cemetery of things long gone....

Dark (K)night

I took a shower in the dark this afternoon
In the twilight I saw the soap you'd left that night
Didn't tell anyone that when you showed up I allowed you to stay
Had to see
Cast my hands over your body aggressively
Shadow-boxed the apology
Fell from the couch to the floor
Moved furnishings
Redecorating
Went to work with bruises on my arm
Someone asked what happened but
You wouldn't ever cause harm that shows itself
Forgot you're just strong
I traced your skin against my will while you slept to see if it still felt like
chocolate and silk and it did
But it was tainted
Knew her fingertips had traipsed across the paths I'd excavated
But she can walk across you barefoot and I'd worn boots
There were thorns here before
I cleared them
With sling blade and spoon
Knew you needed me now but you've grown too elusive
Saw your soap in a green box on the bath's ledge while I stood surrounded
by steam and the melody of drops splashing the basin
Striking me
I saw the metaphor clearly
They seek me to be cleaned
To pick their teeth
To rinse off the chaos
Then leave
Leave me the debris
And the shrapnel
And the unwrapping
Didn't tell them I couldn't even look at you
Wouldn't cook for you

Didn't hug you
Couldn't sit still
Kept my arms crossed unless we were tussling
You mentioned noticing I was using all my strength
You held me that night
Pulled me into you
Kept feeling me leave though I couldn't fall asleep
Not in your clutch
It was no longer comfortable
It wasn't for me
You needed cleaning
I was a pumice stone for your mistakes
My stem has grown thorns these last 6 months
I try to prick you and remember this has been harder on you so there's
nothing I can concoct to harm you
When you leave here it will rain on your head again
You sought solace on my doorstep but you found anger and resentment
Took my abuse because you now feel as if you deserve it
But I am not a harborer of fists and dark words
It overtakes you
Knew you were coming for abuse
You cared not with your overnight bag and raw food
I made you prepare your own meal
I'm not honored now
You struggled through the spice cabinet and I watched with joy so dark
I questioned my heart
While I fake folded laundry in the closet
But you did it
You have been surviving without me
Why are you here?
The dog tried to mediate
He was angry when I started to punch you
He knows this is not me
He knows that there is something off within your body
But I refuse to be wrench and Allen key
Against my wishes he perched on your chest
He is of me
And will absorb things that won't stick to him
Write them off to repel them

He always loved you
I heard you wake and prepare me for your departure
As if you'd be back
You wouldn't
I won't allow you this time
I watched you dress
An obsidian sculpture
But you've got cracks now
Still beautiful
Revoking your admission on my canvas though
Gotta unlearn this despair
Unlearn the brush strokes that got me here
You walked away and I prayed behind your back
But this time my hand didn't find itself on your shoulder
I stood there in my underwear as you promised to talk to me later
This time I didn't care...
Goodbye, dark (k)night.

<u>Beignet</u>

He had the sting of powdered sugar to the throat when you lack mastery
in your method of eating beignets
Even sweet things are dangerous

LIttle Monsters Everywhere

We create these monsters,
And we're never quite open to slaying them.
We contract killers to alleviate the problems then
feel as if the punishments are too cruel & unusual so we admonish them.
Instantly morphing the confidant into the villain.
Charged with the atrocity of putting critical thinking skills to use.
To assist you...
in subduing the big brown eyed beast that's been feeding at your teat
since it's
inception.
Since the conception of the thought that you could save this creature and
teach it to be a
reflection of you.
When realistically, the only image of you it sees in itself is when laying
eggs in your
pool.
Unfortunately, the mother of the mosquito is you.
So refrain from scratching the bite.
Avoid bandaging the lacerations at all costs and throw caution to the
thought that you
were immune to the slight.
We create these malignant horrors.
Born of noxious bellies and nurtured with the milk of gentle hands & pity.
My my aren't the bands of the snake pretty?
So patiently painted with vibrant hue.

4
HURACÁN

8 Little Prayers

I.

And lately,
Mornings have drunkenly stumbled upon me... angrily
Managing to rap to me succinctly about good times that really didn't exist
outside of my musings and imagining
See, in my wildest dreams...
You come back.
Grappling through slurred speech and spinning ceilings
Bamming foolishly on my door trying to inextricably unfuck our things
Reaching.

II.

Why are your fists clenched?
Why are you shaking?
My runaway baby.

III.

Awakening.
Wet dreams have taken shapelessness like paralysis of sleep
And now thoughts of you have a tendency to unfurl a toothy grin into a
broken vee...
What a long face one must have for the corners of a frown to fall that
deep,
And by Tuesday of that week,
I'd crafted barbed wire and peace into catchers of my dreams
I'd placed them in the windows.
I'd hung one above my bed.
I'd clasped my hands and asked if they may protect my head while I rest
I'd protested your spirit-visits to my nest with wild-eye, stomp, and yell
I'd decided you must be ruing the day that you gathered your thing and
left

Unannounced.
And proud.

IV.

The next night by AM quarter of four,
With Venus fly-traps I'd lined the floor.
I'd called on God and chanted
I don't
I don't
From the automobile to the job to the store to the hole I'd tirelessly stared
into the floor
I don't
I don't
From the shower to the show to the sanctuary to the kitchen it was made
ritual to mention
I don't
I don't
Want you no more
Amen.
But the heart keeps calling
Heart keeps stalling
Heart keeps young in the midst of my mane graying
This hand
And fingertips
This pen that I've kept you alive with
I don't
I don't
Amen.

V.

Into the night I drifted...
Having sang song and prayed the liberation of the space you reside in
Kindly, get out.
I've gotta make room in the storehouse.
By Friday at sundown I'd swept the doorway
With a whisk fashioned from déjà senti and what we could've been
I'd used the remains of paper adorning the box of vanish you'd left as a

parting gift to cover the vents to prevent you from slipping back in
I don't
I don't

VI.

I was saging the temple and folding the linens by the evening of the
sabbath
Honored the twilight by eating a late snack of your favorite foods to
summon you through
I slept upright that night in your favorite corner of my room

VII.

I waited for you.

VIII.

This will not be romantic.
In case it is though,
I can't help it.
In my wildest dreams you come back and
I've written every version of you with the exception of the one that
existed
This will not be romantic
Just know this,
In case it is though,
You might consider me different.

Picture me
Last scene, last seen, leaving flowers on your grave before I wake.
I gave.
And I bathed,
In the soot of your aftermaths
You flightless phoenix

I don't
I don't

Amen.

Huracán

And really,

That's where I met her...

In a wet box.

It was hot.

It was nothing like meeting a stranger though, ya know?

It was like 'hey, do I know you?...'

And she replied

'It's nice to meet you too',

But no one else was in the room.

In a wet box.

One of us had on shoes,

The other wore wet socks.

It was also hot.

Smelled real funny,

Smelled like omg and a lot,

Smelled like what the fuck and road block,

Smelled like I just left,

Smelled like drowning & rot,

Smelled like...

Stop.

Like shock like,

The aroma of your chest underneath a pile of rocks.

Like shock like

The aroma of your chest underneath Tupperware containing the trinkets of your life,

No bleeding.

Just debris,

Just deep squeeze.

And.

Heat.

This is where she and I meet.

She said,

'Just keep moving, let this thing be'

And,

This was an inopportune time to believe but,

I've gotta listen 'cause,

Ever since I walked through that door she's been acting like she really knows me

In this,

Wet box

Wet box.

She just stood and watched over me,

From room to car to window to porch,

Just hoisting my shit into the grass

Throwing all my poor shit away 'cause it was too wet, too gone to pack

Never asked her to help...

I got the idea she wasn't there for that.

She was there to shove her fingers in the cracks,

She was there to bolt rampart to my back,

She just stood and paid me racks on racks of heed,

Handed me the same tissue for my eyes she'd used to wipe my slate clean,

Said she was giving me a gift before I leave.

Hand on back,

Pushing thee,

Occupying passenger seat,

Reaching over and

Steering,

Keeping people out of the street for me,

I was looking but frankly couldn't see,

My mouth moving,

She handled speaking,

God puppeteer,

She string,

I'm dancing,

Justa' tryin to stay on beat.

There was no electricity.

Felt like a foot race,

Concrete,

Bare feet

She and I and the sun racing west down Harrison Street.

'I will not impress you here',

I told her,

Bent over with hands coffee-broken on knees,

'I'm starting to dwindle,

Pieces of me are laying in the yard,

I'm lying in the kitchen,

I'm lying in the closet,

in Winter's room with suitcases and my hunger on this devoured mission,

I feel eaten and savagely swallowed,

I'm lying face-down in the back of this thing's throat,

Waiting for its tongue to roll me over

I cannot,

Impress you here, dear-whoever-you-are'

And really, THIS is where she and I meet:

Middle of Harrison Street

Sun-down

I now

Mildewed and sticky like she,

This wraithy thing,

Height-adjacent, tattooed, & full-bellied,

Brule-brown, bulletproof, & foolhardy

She

Donned an electrifyingly familiar gap in her teeth,

Looking like a direct descendant of June & Emma Pea,

She

Matter-of-factly revealed to me

That she was staying here but it was time for me to leave,

Said,

She embedded tragedy in my feet.

Said if I stay too long contentment would severely disfigure my fortè and
my deed

Said she was well-versed in these things,

Told me I had 2 minutes to get in the car and leave,

I still had questions,

She left,

She walked away from me.

Wet socks.

She was going back into the wet box,

It was so hot.

Smelled real funny,

Smelled like 11:59 & deadline

Smelled like mold & honey,

Before she stirred off in the dark,

'Who was she?'

About-faced in the doorframe

I realized,

She was me....

Psalm 30:5

"Weeping may endure for a night, but joy cometh in the morning."

-Psalm 30:5

Weeping may endure for a night,

And it's been dark for what feels like ages

And my face,

My face is raw

And burning

Yearning for some sunlight

For things to get something close to right

Can't see the good things that occur in between all the calamity and sheen of unsightly scenes and weaponry

If it ain't my body it's my material things

Leaving from me

If it ain't my love it's the embodiment of he

Leaving from me

Abruptly

Can see

It's dark

Eyes blinded by the stuck pieces of shirt sleeve

And palm

And fingers that have dried in the last few minutes since their last swipe at my under eye

And cheek

I weep

Silently

Wanna be strong, presenting

I suffer.... peacefully

Can't lay on my stomach

Can't lay on my chest

Can't lay on my back

Everything aches

Can't be portrayed as weak

So I don't speak

I weep

When no one is looking

And night is lasting long

I've yet to be strong

I just keep

I just keep

I just keep

Going

Energizer

On fumes but I keep running

I am tired saxophone

And lazy tympani

Thunderous lagging

Can't pick up my feet

I'm fine fine

Tonight I'll be weeping

It's been dark for ages now

They say joy might come in the morning

But my sun must be broken

My sun broke on me suddenly

Just one day it was real real bright

And then in a flash and bang and a ol heavy ol rain

Just a big ol bang

Pulled the rug out from under me

Me and ol Harrison street

It was there that I started to weep

Night certainly fell upon me

Enduring

But they say joy....

They say joy...

Hopefully it comes with Morning

Earthquake

My landscape agitates, without premonition

My landscape agitates,

I wondered if it'd stop shaking in a minute...

Wondered if I just kept... moving & refused to keep still then... maybe I wouldn't fall in

In the movement

The streets keep movin.

Walls keep sliding

Sky keep falling and everybody's calling

And I'm stalling,

Stuck stuttering attempting to conceive what just happened

And these sinkholes seem to swallow everything, things, everything, me, everything, he, everything, not really, everything, I didn't need, everything, clearing path for me, everything, is anybody seeing this?

Everything

I'm trembling and can't seem to stop these

Tremors, got everything moving

Its 1989 San Francisco again,

I was a kid,

When the shaking of the ground broke that bridge

I was a kid,

Watching from the windowsill,

But the magnitude of it wasn't shit for the building I was standing in,

But the magnitude of it was no match for the home we lived in,

Home alone in a second-story flat modified to withstand it

I never saw anything like that again until I felt the makings of a new groove within

My landscape agitates, without any premonition

My landscape agitates,

I wondered if it'd stop shaking in a minute...

Wondered if I just kept... moving & refused to keep still then... maybe I wouldn't fall in

In the movement

The streets keep movin.

Ain't gotta look down to see things crumbling beneath

Humbling and planting seeds falling in the seams I can't yet see cuz these

Richter scale readings strong enough to topple the complex collection of things I haven't dealt with yet

Caught in the middle of a Tetris type of squeeze

Blunt objects and things, plummeting toward my head and I can't seem to plant my feet

I keep tryin to fall to my knees

Everybody watching without hands wide enough to catch me

But my village full of fishermen

Casting nets between me and the cracks to aid and abed my scarred feet
while I was asleep

Just

Brace me

In the middle of the cascading

These cracks in the street have mouths that keep opening to show me its
teeth

I wondered if it'd stop shaking in a minute...

Wondered if I just kept... walking & thought to keep talkin then... maybe I
wouldn't fall in

In the movement

The streets keep movin

My landscape agitates, without any premonition

My landscape agitates, making

Crush Velvet

I wore him like crushed velvet...

But it was always summer on my skin.

A gentle pressure relentlessly applied,

But I always heard music in the friction between me and his fabric.

I'll never forget it,

It was rhythm & blues that evanescence into a bridge lazily baptized in a decrescendo of second-line trombones and battle axes plummeting to their deaths

I'd consider it the magnum opus of many men

Many, many, many, many men...

There was hallelujah and amen from the chorus as sweat dripped from the crevices of my places and sometimes down my chin

He chafed me often.

And often,

I rang him out like evening's wash-rag before putting my feet back in,

Rang him clockwise like Dali would've envisioned hoping for an oil to spring forth for treatment of the discomfort and the itches that he'd inflicted,

Rang him, because I'd become drenched & heavy too.

Walking each block swimming in my own pool of predicament,

Luxuriating in the very ensemble I'd soon roll tightly and tuck neatly into my carried baggage,

Perhaps, soaking through and through my favorite outfit.

It was summertime and he, Crushed Velvet...

Always had me hot.

And fanning.

Like a southern grandmother demanding that I,

"Take that ol' hot ass dress off, gal!"

Though, Nana doesn't understand that I'm a surrealist in the pursuit of persistence,

A gender-specific form of entertainment fashioned specifically for the little boy sunken within men,

Not to mention

I'm an artist and I'm sensitive about my suffering...

Hence, I, Summertime, with a velvet cloak crust

Encrusted in calico and it's not the only thing that's crushed

He served as the breaker of my bones, invisible cast, and my crutch.

Couldn't fatten my frame in spite of being gluttonous

Kept me dehydrated and sick...

And hungry,

Discomforted

I wore my suicide-mission...

Prohibited my own lips from the stormy kiss of quenched thirst

My outfit was all-consuming and

I couldn't help but wonder if he'd even said his grace first...

Generate

I'm all war and no peace,

I'll never go to war without my piece,

Albeit, lately, I've been in a wading pool of wait a minute...

Trying to make a move

Trying to stage a ballyhoo

But things camouflaged as rock-skipped ripples keep making expertly
executed moves to slow me

Mere puddles in my sea

See, but,

Picture me, generating my kick, from the knee

Finish line crossing having gotten over the gravity of things underneath
the pull of a different moon

Just want my inner voice to say

"nobody... super like you...

Nobody full

No walk

Or alterer of mood,

No eclipse

No Half

Or Quarter

No Wolf big bad enough to bay at your blue"

And I wanna believe it too

Wanna see the fruition all the way through

Sucking the journey across my teeth

And just...breathe

Mere puddles in my sea

See, but,

Picture me, generating my kick, from the knee

<u>5</u>

WHATEVER BDSM MEANS
& OTHER NERD EROTICA

Touching

Traced. Like rain drops caught in the act of defacing window panes they,

Drip. Down. Slowly.

Leaving a messy trail of aftermath from storm, yes it poured

There was thunder, you were Thor.

Reverie. Soft fingertip collision on neck, nape, shoulder, blade, spine, triceps, ass, ribs, ink, scar, chest, up & descend,

Vermillion, Lower lip, forefinger strokes around the rim, your mouth, is that tongue tip? you tried to lick me, soft and pappy though he is king, velvety & mean

Ceiling fan...gently slaying stillness like dragons

Pieces of the wind falling to rest on this plane of man, drizzle of draft falls like dew on your skin, falls like sparks from Roman candle through a summer's night thickness, you're getting hotter now, this is friction, falls like, falls

Eyelids, fist-fighting drowsy, but you like to fight right?

Brown skin, w/ salt water toffee, Hershey's kiss with nut, peppermint stick

Packaged in dress that is pressed but underneath is beast, let him sleep

Please, allow me to unwrap, oh I like gifts, Christmas, wrapper & candies, tissue paper and delicacies, how does yours taste?

Traipse across anatomy, this is only touch, very much gas & clutch, I whisper obscenities, and you bequeath in chuckle and throb

Scribble graffiti all over your body with thumb and pinky, I wish, you could see, I've Henri Mattised it, Georgia O'Keefed you, Da Vinci, & Dali,

I have fucked around & master-pieced and antique

Worthy & sweet, nilla wafer sheen on a dented trophy, he is fast asleep now, this...this is only touching.

Chopped & Screwed

When he strokes from the back I spit poetry rather than say "daddy".

He shifts my uterus making it produce lyrics

I lay rhymes over his exhales

Flashing back to orgasmic raps before 8 tracks were antiquated, I use these mics as foreplay cuz he loves it when I'm flowin and masturbatin

Everytime he presses play the parental advisory is engaged cuz ain't no telling what I'm gonna say I

Secrete these soliloquies copywritten & trademarked in his name

He be, memorizing the throb of my g-spot pre-cum

I, ride in 3/4 time like tap tippy tippy tap tippy tippy tap ratta tat tat

He's a ghostwriter, penetrating deeply pressing against vocal chords while he records

I spit the words that drip from the tip of his pen written on diaphragm, I am pad but he

Bleeds me, reverse of cycles in biology

I am vinyl, 45 to be exact and he...

He's the needle and the scratch in the back

He's dynamic like air appearing out of nowhere to provide a slight gism for your ears to create melodies

He's similar to a blind man's finger tips delicately tickling ivories

He be touching me....

He's sweet like tata pie and ice cream...

Raw & uncut like b.i.g pre Sean C...

He be listening to me...

With his favorite track on repeat...

He is composer, I be symphony

I chop chop and he screw screw screw screws me

And apparently, he said if my mouth is capable of spitting the way it do

Then the lips down there can't do shit but speak the truth too so we converse a lot

And yea...he loves Becky too

So I give him Sonnet

Stanzas pop-locked & spit-shined straight off the top of my bonnet

I am synonymous with dome, I give him that good good good knowledge

Bands

It is dark,
and a rogue streak of light from the parking lot has somehow forced its
way through the curtains
Tagging his body with graffiti
In the likeness of tiger stripes...
Or maybe lightening bolts depending on the imagination.
He is long and trim yet
The evidence of finding pleasure in an occasional feast of fried delicacies &
liquor is barely there
And while jealousy is not a trait that my personality has ever given
residency,
Envy pulses through my joints at the look of satisfaction seemingly felt
By the band of his boxer briefs just....resting there
Looking traceable,
With my thumb & forefinger
With my tongue
Whichever he suggests
That band just rests there...
Safely below the navel,
Nestled in happy-trail,
Hitting perpendicularly that "V",
He has angles, see...
That street lamp is on my team,
Creeping through the shades sectioning him off so righteously
But the horizon created by skin having flowed once so effortlessly being
blatantly cut off by the band of this...
Boxer brief
Masterpiece
Jesus peace
Pardon me...
Shadow and light suggest that the fabric whose sole purpose was to serve
as a covering for the crotch
Has, in it's own zest for life,
Challenged his cock to a duel & at any given moment
One of them will lose
Yet the band....
Is so calm,
And confidant,

Poised,
Attractive,
Relevant.
Lowering blood pressure & slowed breathing indicate that I may be
pushed into confrontation with my new arch nemesis
Which...is unfortunate
I will be steadfast in my approach
Because this is not a place for rushing.
For a moment my hands become tigers too passing through soft blazes of
light down his belly
As fingertips,
& light scratches against the hips,
Coupled with a little pressure on the grab & pull-back must work in unison
This is the pagan meaning of Christmas,
And behind this fragile mesh is a gift...

Intruder

You show up naked and expect me to cover my eyes...
& I've peeped through the cracks between my fingers so long
That everything i see is shaped like the quarter moon,
Everything stays dark,
Even at 1/2 past noon.
You show up nude...
Daring me.
to not.
be turned on.
This is submission,
You point,
And I listen.
Here he is, ladies & gents
The Alchemist with the hand signals,
And I've got a keen sense of comprehension when it involves your
mannerisms
It's calling,
Tripping & silent alarming,
Like rat traps that clap back in slow motion
Whispering "WHAM".........
Just before the slam
But it's...
It's the tremors that get you...
The shaking of a limb,
The flushing of a lip,
The slow pressure around the neck from a hand with purposed grip,
Expansive and delicate.
A soft quaking beneath pinches of skin that you never knew existed until it
quivered,
Quickly,
Unsure if I can even swim in this deep...
A voyeur to my own secrecies...
A peeper in my own feature,
I spy from behind the quarter moon

I am uzi
I am hair-pin trigger,
And you are confident that I am not a killer but...

Palmetto & Whiskey

I kept taking stabs at composing those last two chapter passages about the thing, sweetly.
But my failed attempts only carved murderous rips into my manuscript's remaining sheets
Metaphorically, of yours it reminded me…
The place where patience had been held sometimes, without ransom, folded blind by candlelight, but plentily fed
Left wet, twisted, amongst our legs bunched between
Disheveled discreetly in the umbra of the kitchen light and tv
Exacerbating passion both angrily and meek
Speaking to me raspy and deep
This one meant something.
And the one directly following.
In addition to the next several
Consecutive.
Sentences of intimacy.
Consequential.
Intentional.
I heard ringing folklorically in my head once you finished passing down unwritten stories through me orally.
Emptied my aqueduct thoroughly never failing to return from your swim each time with a kiss,
Without incident, sharing the last remnant of honey wine from this time in my cellar that you'd dug up
Mix-tapes ruminated repeatedly from a far corner of the frame in sync with my breaths that hinged on the cusp of your drum.
I inherited new culture from the cup of your tongue,
Gently bounced on the tip to the flicker of darkness
And now my skin is fitting different.
In all things I keep striving to list the characteristics of the experience but the words only trickle from my finger tips in scribble.
Around here we eat inaccurate depictions of the illicit for breakfast with aspirations of reflecting back on the tryst by dinner with precision,
Feasting at the chef's table overrun by single-servings of you.

It must be more than just raunchy ricochets of dirty stanzas ending in 'dick'
for emphasis read in crowded rooms with underwhelming lyricists
Allowed to live another night, another mic with projection and acoustics in
tow to woo the audience,
This is glacé taboo.
Candied yam on the palette,
Inherently dirty and deep root,
Consumed with internal juke,
I always liked to dance with my food.
I wanna craft more bars for this music than America's privatized prison
systems, but sweetly.
Yet these crumpled beginnings and excerpts having failed to launch lay folded
over in piles
While the contention between my pen and I multiplies
Strategizing how to dissertate your drip with efficacy & style,
Like you do,
A loose leaf aloof piece,
The composition must've been well above my paygrade and a higher cost of
living than the loft on my writer's block
I'm no stranger to taking in foxtrots with the erotic,
With license to jiggle all of the genres in my pocket
Cat-calling in different octaves
Fluent in haiku and sonnet.
I've been an architect of metaphors meant for conjuring up flush.
And cheek blush.
And slow pacing tsunamis of rushed blood that didn't accost anyone's mind
until I'd made it to the next line
But you,
Needed to be unlikely erotica.
An inverted depiction of the typical when the finished product is better than
the experience.
Having unpacked the intricacies of intimacy from their plastic bag for which
there were no holes to breathe.
Every fistful of beginnings lacked erogenous tones
With consideration lent to misguided lapses in judgment while adapting to
your absence,
It still needed to thump,
And titillate.
The words needed to nestle and lay nicking nipples gently with its teeth.

Needing to flick strips of leather from the wrist popping from the paper,
Sounding off like the impact of your hands on my ass when you really mean it
It needed to be herbaceous in nature,
Needed to describe Tobacco Blossom & whiskey,
Without using 'like' or 'as',
So, I kept taking stabs at composing those last two chapter passages about the
thing, sweetly.
But my failed attempts only carved murderous rips into my manuscript's
remaining sheets
Metaphorically, of yours it reminded me...

Printed in Poland
by Amazon Fulfillment
Poland Sp. z o.o., Wrocław

59926189R00058